THE SPACE BETWEEN

Poetry
by
J.R. Brady

Beatitude PRESS
BERKELEY, CALIFORNIA

Book and Cover Designed by Douglas Rees

Published in the United States of America
By Beatitude Press, Berkeley, California
All rights reserved.
Printed by 1984 Printing in Oakland, California

ISBN: 978-0-9825066-6-0

For Jon

Contents

ACKNOWLEDGMENTS

Thanks is given to...

THE TYPEWRITER for publication of *Bat Sense*.

THE SAN FRANCISCO BAY GUARDIAN for its poetry competition finalist awards to *Generations* and *Two Women*.

THE 3300 REVIEW for publication of *The Commuter*.

OXYGEN for publication of *An Applicant Contemplates Louise Brooks*.

NORTH BEACH JOURNAL for publication of *Justice* and *After Yeats*.

NORTH COAST LITERARY REVIEW for publication of *The Priestess*, *After Yeats* and *Loch Ness*.

Additionally: *Loch Ness* has a history of a drama/short-play award and two stage productions.

ABOVE
THE
WATER

BAT SENSE

Studies show that when
a bat is put into
a refrigerator
it instantly will begin
to hibernate...but then
as soon as it is warm
it will revive again unharmed.

How often I have wished
that I could sleep like that
except for summer nights
filled with stars.

GENERATIONS

When my grandmother left her last
husband...she moved to the desert...and lived
by herself in a trailer...and smoked
tipperillos...and drank whiskey and sat
outside on hot...dark nights studying
the stars...till she knew the constellations
better than the children she had born...
while embraced in younger passions...passing...
by vanished...unmissed men. I met her once...
and sat with her in the dark...and she showed me
the night...and the north star...and the big dipper...
distant...in the sky...but then the whiskey
made her mean...and so I cried...alone...
until my mother finally came...and took me home.

DOOLIN
(County Clare, Ireland)

Through a window
        I see her sitting
                In her bookstore of

books that happened
        like strangers, like me
                in a place on the road
                between places

reading, an old woman
        head bent down

(Are customers a distraction?)

Beside her, a calico cat
        sits...washes it's face
                beyond, through an open door

a room full of paintings
        colors dust dull through the window
                browns...gray with soft edges

reality an apparition
        step inside & I
                could be left behind

(Tour buses never wait.)

in this map forgotten place...a stop
        to eat, drink, pee...then
                move on to what is important

Not her & yes her
        always left behind with
                the books...how did they get there?

Step inside & it is...
        a collapse of centuries.

Will I be left behind?
        Will I care?...Would
                she even look up?

What question might I ask?
        Could she transform &
                step out as me & ride off

a tourist carrying away
        my reality

while I...
        fill her cat's milk dish
                settle into her chair

open her book & know
        what came before...new memory,
                new being...while she

muses over the number of travelers checks
        left...& looks at the map to know direction.

New bodies. New lives.
        Your place, my place
                your history here among the

whispered stories of Cuculian & Mave,
        of banshee, of famine, of blood, of stone

(How many tears?)

of time measured in circles of the sun,
        of swans returning in winter...then
            disappearing to return again...
            to wetlands, bogs & stone...&

Will you remember what you left
        behind in dreams as I finish your book
            allowing the whole of what I gave you
            to vanish...into larger measure.

(Do we care more when the view is smaller?)

Hope you like California & take
        good care of the cat...
            as I will yours.

COMMUTER

I.

temp-job lunch in unseasonal heat
& today I walk to the waterfront
with newspaper, diet coke & take-out tuna
packed fresh in disposable plastic wrap
past cafe tables filled with people
paying...for fast service...

down to a bench by rocks & water
& as I eat...I read...of causalities & greed
& promises that...prosperity is just around the corner

& I try to recall the songs we sang
back when we still...believed in something
but I can't...because I keep thinking of
this thirteen-year-old kid I know
who wants to die...but won't say why
& how last month...when he cut his wrists
the hospital gave him ten stitches & Prozac

years ago, I remember how he made himself a tail
& pretended he was a dinosaur
& his first grade teacher called up concerned
because...he wouldn't stop crying
after he was told...dinosaurs were extinct

now he says...he won't go to school anymore
& instead of trying to kill himself
he steals & runs away...

I think he is better.

II.

a gull settles near me on a rock
hoping for leftovers he won't get
because he doesn't like diet coke &
the rest is finished...so off he flies...low
over the water...climbing steadily...toward the sun

when I was a child, I used to say
I wanted to live with the birds
now I ride home through tunnels
more & more I ride through the tunnels
it is faster...but sometimes...

I miss seeing things...in between

AN APPLICANT CONTEMPLATES
LOUISE BROOKS

"Go in and get them."
It's an old man's voice.
I can't see him but I know he is there
hidden somewhere amid
soft leather and philodendrons.

There is this thing about looking for a job.
You wind up places you never
imagined you would be.
Resume, briefcase, waiting places
filled with soft leather and philodendrons.

I wouldn't have thought about it, so much
if it hadn't been for the picture of Louise Brooks...
Silent movie star remembered.
Time caught. Flapper caught.
Dark eyes with black hair helmet
in velvets, silks and ropes of pearls
standing in a shadowed
piano-playing room
that might have smelled
of opium and alcohol and perfume.

"No mercy," says the old man.
"Let them get away with it once
and they just keep coming back.
No mercy. It's the only way."

And in the magazine it says
that once upon a time
Louise Brooks was born beautiful
and danced for...Denishawn and Ziegfied
and made silent movies
whenever it was that she wasn't reading
more books than a woman should
or telling important people what she really thought
(even when she wasn't drunk)
or...when it was that she wasn't loving
first Chaplin...then Garbo
with a personal kind of passion
that rendered gender incidental.

And so...she...repeatedly...got herself
thrown out of wherever she was
till she wound up working
for a New York escort service which
wasn't like being a prostitute...she said
but no one believed her.

And I freeze in my waiting
and I wonder...do I have an extra resume
because I can't get a job without a resume...

but I know I am past being hunted
because I say all the right words
and...always I sit with my knees together
and 1 am here instead of there
in this place that I don't want to be
surrounded by soft leather and philodendrons
and I know all is right with the world
and I wonder how in the hell
it ever got to be that way.

"No mercy," says the old man
"We should do like we did in World War II.
Just go in and wipe them out ...
Just like World War II."

And then there's Louise Brooks
who I know is a them.

And I wonder about the old man
and if he ever...touched...or loved...or
dreamed of things that weren't allowed
and what if...before he got
the chance to "wipe her out"

Louise Brooks had said to him
"hey old man, let's screw instead"
and if he would...or if he could
maybe it would have been nothing...or
maybe it would have been everything
past his far side of darkness
and instead of there being a war
they might have been movie stars together...

like Lucy and Desi
or Punch and Judy
or Adam and Eve...

but there is no place else...visible...
and I wish someone would call my name
for I need to say how much it is
I want to be what I'm not
because if I don't soon they might find out
that my resume is wrinkled
and my pantyhose itch
and my knees ache
and I hate soft leather and philodendrons

and the old man for making me afraid
of places dreamed past certainty
where light and shadow dance connected
with no way back...ever...

For then I would be left
lost in a world of should-shrouded selves
forever noticed, forever wondered about
always seeking the invisible
not because I don't care, but because I do
never knowing when it is I will be told
I am not what it was they expected me to be
until I wind up just like Louise Brooks...

who loved the feel of velvet
and silk, and perfume
and so many books
and the touch of those she wanted
never asking...did they want her more
than she wanted them...

and who...in aloneness...held tight
to philosophers' words...and poet's songs
"And who knows," they said,
"what she might have been
if her times had let her"...

and who...in the end...died old
in the company of a friend...
never caring...that she was remembered.

JUSTICE

Reconciliation
inspiration...
gravity...

The lion lies
with the lamb
surrounded by
approving creatures.

Tonight he will want dinner.

It is all temporary
a place to perch
a ledge without wind
another identity
a metamorphosis
of ancient enemies.

In the night...a howling
wolves
coyotes
banshee
an ambulance...
on the ground...
shattered glass.

Released...a canary sings
on a telephone wire
while the white cockatoo
heads for Miami
where the food is better
for his kind.

The rain forest was too far.

"Is it still there?" I ask
the bartender who
is studying to be a lawyer
on his days off.

BELOW
THE
WATER

THE PRIESTESS

White moths circle
A globe
Of blue light.

Beer gone flat
In a cracked glass.

A crescent moon
Ending.

The sound of a guitar.

I dream of Atlantis
While astronomers count the stars.

In another life
I think I mattered.

A huntress perhaps
In the century of light?

The fire has burned so long
I can hardly see it

There is a great
Loneliness
In this space...

Between necessity...and magic.

THE EMPRESS

I have a compulsion
To open doors
To let in spiders and sunlight

Once, I spun straw into gold
But it changed back
Turning the treasury into a stable

By then
All the story people wanted to hear
Had ended

My pale sister says
I should stop listening

I envy her
She lives luminescent
In her own galaxy
Of alcohol and gardenias

Mine is the place
Where princes lie
Happily
In the beds of their mistresses

And princesses breed quietly
Or die violently
Looking for a life

Me, I prefer stuffed duck
And warm rooms
To promises of affection

Better to endure
A cracked violin
Than miss the dance

TWO WOMEN
(for Berta)

You gave me your mirror when you died...
& I wondered why
       because I only knew you at distances.

You were a woman of my mother's world...
my mother's generation
       a believing in...being there for kind of woman...
       caught between moments of fury...& despair
       a woman counted among women...who
       lived behind men who lived...on the edge
       of politics...of art...of themselves...
       men who quoted Hemingway & Sandberg
& Karl Marx...
       men who all knew Diego Rivera...
but never mentioned Frida...
       men who took the fifth amendment
& lost jobs & went to jail...
       men who drank too much & slept around...
       men who lived out half-made dreams...lost in red
       sunsets...men...who never stopped believing.

& I think about what my mother used to tell me
       about what you were like...way back...before
       I was born...back in the depression years.

About how you came from Mexico to San Francisco...
       about how you worked as a Sinaloa cigarette girl...
       about how you were beautiful...about how
       your husband pursued you & pursued you
       until you finally agreed to marry him...&
       about how everyone was so surprised when
       you finally did...& about how much more he
       loved you than you loved him...in the beginning.

& I remember how...once...I saw you crying at
            a party in nineteen-fifty-three...& how
            I picked up the marigold that had fallen
            from your hair & gave it back to you...&
            how you hugged me...& wrapped me up
            in your red shawl & told me I should always wear red
            because red is the color of the sun.

& I remember how other women liked you...& how
            all of you would sit together...long kitchen hours...
        smoking...&
            drinking wine...& talking about how...
        so often...feelings did seem
            just as important as economics...
        even if they weren't logical.

& I wonder about you...& if your life was really better after your
            husband became rich...instead of famous...
        like he wanted...&
            did you ever stop hoping your lost son
        would come back...or
            was your other son (the one who gave
        you grandchildren)
            finally enough...& did you...like my mother...so often
            think about leaving...but never did.

& then I think of how...once...l told you...l don't like men who
            make me cry...& staying whole seems easier...when
            I'm alone...& how you said that none of it was easy
            but none of it was dull either...
        & I wonder if...perhaps...
            that is the most anyone can wish for...

& I look in your mirror...& I see myself...& I see you
in your red shawl...& I think about how death
touches life...&
about how much I wish I could have known
you...back then...
in your revolution waiting kitchen hours...
& I think of death.. &
of those almost winter nights...
when souls move freely...safe
upon the earth...& I think of how I now will
welcome them...&
in their darkness...spread for you a path
of marigolds...so
you may find me waiting...with lighted candles.

& we will sit together...& smoke & drink fine wine
& you will tell me
who it was that you first loved...
when you were young in Çuernavaca
& I will tell you of my Irish dead...
& of my own love...lost too soon...
& how much it is I need for them to know
that I am well...&
together we will wonder at a world
so long uncertain...&
together we will talk of how it is that things that
don't make sense
always matter most...& together we will find in
each our own
lost selves...held safe within the space made
warm between us
long...long...long...before our morning's....separation
....of the sun.

AFTER YEATS

Come away, O'human child
To the waters & the wild...
For the world's more full of wheeping
Than you can understand

Yeats (The Stolen Child)

Changeling, marked & measured
wrapped in old blankets
waking to strange light...in
spaces not counted in dreams...

"why me," it said...
they knew as soon as I was born...
yet could not say the difference...
other than...suddenly...I was...
disappointing...even though
I grew in balanced proportions &
was attentive when spoken to...

at least the shell...the inside was
still my own...too dark the eyes...
too quick the tongue...& the
silence...unbearable to them...

grown...released...
"no place here for this" they said...
& so I wait...left on a highway...
without footprints or horizon...
trying to thumb a ride...&...

the world's more full of wheeping
than you can understand.

PERSEPHONE

The pomegranate juice has stained my fingers.
Its sweetness lingers deep inside my mouth.
In darkness I crave the taste of sweet fruit
as once...I only craved the sun...and
my hunger keeps me safe from rescue
deep in this place of unmentionable dreams.

My mother claims I was carried here screaming
but that is her lie...a lie needed to mourn a 'child'
of assumed virtue....and to justify what followed.

The truth is...it began with wildflowers...
the iris...the lily...the narcissus...
all pulled from their damp earth
and clung to in fragrant armfuls.
Often...I had been cautioned against taking
so many...but...back then they were uncountable.

When first I saw him...
he was riding a black horse...
heavy with sweat that dripped from
a bit pulled tight against its mouth.
I remember how he sat...quietly
watching...as I told him I could see
the animal had been driven too hard.

I never asked...but when he offered his hand
to pull me up in front of him...I took it
willingly...for the stirrup was high and I
knew...I never could have reached it alone.

The rest I remember as a dream...
my hands grasping the saddle...
eyes shut tight against the wind... until...
with a slower pace...the air turned thick and hot...
and I could see we had entered a maze of tunnels...
that wound downward in a dark tangle of directions...
where...easily...we might have lost ourselves
had it not been for the glowing anubis
that ran ahead...as we traveled past
silhouetted figures with narrow...
luminous eyes...their expression strange...but
not unkind....in their curiosity.

The chamber he took me to was warmly lit
by candles set in rock...carved with a multitude of
faces...all more animal than man...and
gently he guided me into its softest part and
offered me wine...black purple in its glass...and

I refused its taste...but not his hands as he
touched me in places where...before...only
I had given myself pleasure...until...at last...
I felt the ripping wetness of my own flesh and
moans became screams...nonstoppable...and
I knew...I was a thing taken...in a world
changed forever...alone with this stranger who
stroked my shoulder...so carefully...as
I told him there was pain in it...and I knew...
this was the beginning of my loving him.

My mother...my lover...
they fought over me...the way
people who posses things fight...
each claiming all I feel to be their own...
while I waited....lost...indecipherable.

I have seen how fruit...when placed too close to fire...
splits open...with insides changed to sugar running out...
except for the pomegranate...brittle in heat...yet
break away its skin with my fingernails...and I find
a moist...swollen interior...to be dug out bit by bit...
till my hands fill with flesh and seeds and dripping juice...
first to be licked away...then spread across my face
around my eyes...a cool wet crimson mask
turned sticky in the heat of knowing...the sun
still holds for me...the full completion of my being.

And finding me thus transformed...they realized...I
would not be kept by one...so I became divided...
ascending...descending...warming the earth with my
presence...until...inevitability...a black horse and
glowing anubis appear...to guide me back to my
less earthly home...leaving winter in my wake
to mark my mother's grief.

I am called many names...
Kora...Proserpina...Persephone...
the destroyer...bringer of birth and death
and I wish it was not so...and often I have
wondered...would I ever have chosen to
leave...if I had seen into possibility?

But back then...I counted myself a small thing
who hardly mattered...and then I did....and now I know...

I have stepped too far beyond the rim of consciousness
to ever deny what I am for other's kindnesses...
and that is the way of it.

THE SPACE BETWEEN

LOCH NESS
(A Pantoum For Two Voices)

SCIENTIST   **MONSTER**
(above the water)   **(below the water)**
may be male or female   **female***

*(*Note: traditionally the Loch Ness Monster is
locally referred to as female.)*

Place: Loch Ness. Scotland   Time: The present

The characters are lit separately.
Neither is aware of the other.

SCIENTIST
Monster sightings have occurred here since 500 A.D.

MONSTER
I have lived beneath the waters of this Loch all of my life.

SCIENTIST
Reports state that the Creature resembles a large salamander.

MONSTER
And always, despite warnings, I have wondered about
things beyond myself...I have lived beneath the waters of this
Loch all of my life.

SCIENTIST
Recent sightings have been claimed by several Benedictine
priests.

MONSTER
And always, despite warnings, I have wondered about things beyond myself.

SCIENTIST
Others include members of a funeral party and a visiting violinist...Recent sightings have been claimed by several Benedictine priests.

MONSTER
Always, I would watch when the land beasts came, heavy-footed and thirsty.

SCIENTIST
Others include members of funeral party and a visiting violinist.

MONSTER
Before the earthquakes came, before they died, always I would watch them...Always I would watch when the land beasts came, heavy footed and thirsty.

SCIENTIST
All insist her head is eel like, with a long neck.

MONSTER
Before the earthquakes came, before they died, always I would watch them.

SCIENTIST
Her body is said to be large with four flippers and a tail...All insist her head is eel like with a long neck.

MONSTER
I remember how the land split open and I saw them
flailing...screaming.

SCIENTIST
Her body is said to be large with four flippers and a tail.

MONSTER
And everywhere, all around us, was the water and the
boiling heat...I remember how the land split open and I saw
them flailing...screaming.

SCIENTIST
Evidence indicates this description is largely imaginary.

MONSTER
And everywhere, all around us, was the water and the
boiling heat.

SCIENTIST
But recent sonar sightings suggest the presence of something ...
Evidence indicates, this description is largely imaginary.

MONSTER
And I couldn't save them.

SCIENTIST
But...recent sonar sightings suggest the presence of something.

MONSTER
Still, we escaped, swimming deep, deep into watery
caves...and I couldn't save them.

SCIENTIST
There is something larger here than has ever been
recorded before.

MONSTER
Still, we escaped, swimming deep, deep into watery caves.

SCIENTIST
Tracking is arduous. Living tissue is the same density as
water... There is something larger here than has ever been
recorded before.

MONSTER
But I, being the youngest, was small and couldn't swim as fast.

SCIENTIST
Tracking is arduous. Living tissue is the same density as
water.

MONSTER
And so they left me...alone in the darkness...I, being the
youngest, was small and couldn't swim as fast.

SCIENTIST
We doubt the creature is a mammal. She lacks curiosity.

MONSTER
And so they left me, alone in the darkness.

SCIENTIST
We must obtain biological evidence to confirm our
theories...We doubt the creature is a mammal. She lacks
curiosity.

MONSTER
I know I am safe as long as I stay in the caves.

SCIENTIST
We must obtain biological evidence to confirm our theories.

MONSTER
But still I go where the light filters down through the water...I know I am safe as long as I stay in the caves.

SCIENTIST
We have recently acquired electronic harpoons.

MONSTER
But still I go where the light filters down through the water.

SCIENTIST
They are designed to secure adequate biopsy samples...We have acquired electronic harpoons.

MONSTER
And sometimes, when the currents are quiet, I look at the sun.

SCIENTIST
They are designed to secure biopsy samples.

MONSTER
And I see the land has become still again...Sometimes, when the currents are quiet, I look at the sun.

SCIENTIST
We are confident, all wounds inflicted will be minor.

MONSTER
And I see the land has become still again.

SCIENTIST
It is important we explain all biological phenomena...We are confident all wounds inflicted will be minor.

MONSTER
And the beasts have become smaller and less fearful.

SCIENTIST
We must explain all biological phenomena.

MONSTER
It is so lonely in the caves, and I do so long to know of things beyond myself ...And the beasts are smaller and less fearful.

SCIENTIST
Monster sightings have occurred here since 500 A.D.

MONSTER
It is so lonely in the caves...and I do so long to know of things beyond myself.

SCIENTIST
Reports state, the Creature resembles a large salamander.

CURTAIN